Acts

KENNETH O. GANGEL

VICTOR BOOKS®

A DIVISION OF SCRIPTURE PRESS PUBLICATIONS INC.
USA CANADA ENGLAND

Unless otherwise noted, Scripture quotations in this
Bible study are from the *Holy Bible, New International
Version,* ©1973, 1978, 1984, International Bible Soci-
ety. Used by permission of Zondervan Bible Publishers.

Recommended Dewey Decimal Classification: 226.6
Suggested Subject Heading: BIBLE, N.T.—ACTS

Library of Congress Catalog Card Number: 87-81005
ISBN: 0-89693-765-8

VICTOR BOOKS
A division of SP Publications, Inc.
          Wheaton, Illinos 60187

CONTENTS

How to Use This Study   *7*
Introduction to the Acts of the Apostles   *9*

1. **ACTS 1:1-11** *We Are Witnesses*   *13*

2. **ACTS 1:12–2:47** *Beginnings of the Church*   *19*

3. **ACTS 3–5** *Early Ministry in Jerusalem*   *25*

4. **ACTS 6–7** *Stephen and the Six Servants*   *33*

5. **ACTS 8–9** *Three People God Used*   *39*

6. **ACTS 10–12** *Apostolic Adventures*   *45*

7. **ACTS 13–15** *The First Missionary Journey*   *53*

8. **ACTS 16–18:22** *The Second Missionary Journey*   *61*

9. **ACTS 18:23–21:19** *The Third Missionary Journey*   *69*

10. **ACTS 21:20–23:35** *Arrest in Jerusalem*   *77*

11. **ACTS 24–26** *Felix, Festus, and Agrippa*   *85*

12. **ACTS 27–28** *From Caesarea to Rome*   *91*

How to Use This Study

Personal Growth Bible Studies are designed to help you understand God's Word and how it applies to everyday life. To complete the studies in this book, you will need to use a Bible. A good modern translation of the Bible, such as the *New International Version* or the *New American Standard Bible*, will give you the most help. (NOTE: the questions in this book are based on the *New International Version*.)

You will find it helpful to follow a similar sequence with each study. First, read the introductory paragraphs. This material helps set the tone and lay the groundwork for the passage to be studied. Once you have completed this part of the study, spend time reading the assigned passage in your Bible. This will give you a general feel for the content of the passage.

Having completed the preliminaries, you are then ready to dig deeper into the Scripture passage. Each study is divided into several sections so that you can take a close-up look at the smaller parts of the larger passage. These sections each begin with a synopsis of the Scripture to be studied in that section. Following each synopsis is a two-part study section made up of *Explaining the Text* and *Examining the Text*.

Explaining the Text gives background notes and commentary to help you understand points in the text that may not be readily apparent. After reading any comments that appear in *Explaining the Text*, answer each question under *Examining the Text*.

At the end of each study is a section called *Experiencing the Text*. The questions in this section focus on the application of biblical principles to life. You may find that some of the questions can be answered immediately; others will require that you spend more time reflecting on the passages you have just studied.

The distinctive format of the Personal Growth Bible Studies make them easy to use individually as well as for group study. If the majority of those in your group answer the questions before the group meeting, spend most of your time together discussing the *Experiencing* questions. If, on the other hand, members have not answered the questions ahead of time and you have adequate time in your group meeting, work through all of the questions together.

However you use this series of studies, our prayer is that you will understand the Bible as never before, and that because of this understanding, you will experience a rich and dynamic Christian life. If questions of interpretation arise in the course of this study, we recommend you refer to the two-volume set, *The Bible Knowledge Commentary*, edited by John F. Walvoord and Roy B. Zuck (Victor Books, 1984, 1986).

Introduction to the Acts of the Apostles

Hardly "silent," as they are often called, the period of 400 years between the Old and New Testaments was an exciting time in history, as God prepared the world for the coming of the Messiah. As the Old Testament record ends, the Jews are returning to Israel to rebuild both the walls and temple in Jerusalem. This return of the Jews to their homeland was possible because of a decree Cyrus, king of Persia, issued in 538 B.C., the last event described in the Old Testament is Nehemiah's visit to Persia, which ended about 420 B.C.

The next dramatic event to take place in the Near Eastern world was the defeat of the Persian armies by Alexander the Great in 333 B.C. From Asia Minor, Alexander moved east and then south through Syria, Palestine, and Egypt. One historian claims that Alexander so changed the world that nothing after him was ever the same again. The change he was speaking about was primarily cultural, not military.

By the time of Alexander's death, two of the three major pillars upon which New Testament history would be built were in place—the revitalization of Hebrew religion and the spread of Hellenistic (Greek) culture all around the Middle East. But the Ptolemies who attempted to control the Greek Empire after the death of Alexander could not maintain his level of leadership. Nor could their Syrian counterparts, the Seleucids. The major difference between these two branches of the post-Alexandrian empire was that the Ptolmies showed a level of tolerance toward Jewish religion and institutions while the Seleucids were determined to superimpose Hellenism on the Jews.

Enter the villain—Antichus IV, surnamed Epiphanes, who oppressed the Jews to such an extent that he became known as a historical forerunner of the Antichrist.

During the time of Epiphanes, the Jews revolted. This revolt was set off by Mattathias, the priest, and was carried out by his son, Judas Maccabeas ("the hammer"). The revolt was short-lived. The armies of Lysias seized Jerusalem, offered terms of peace which were accepted but later violated by the Greeks, and set off what amounted to a civil war in the second century before Christ.

Then God made ready the third pillar—Roman law and civil government. As the Romans stretched their tentacles of power across the Mediterranean world from west to east, a man by the name of Herod, son of Antipater, won the favor of Anthony and was officially named "King of the Jews." Herod the Great's rule lasted 33 years, from 37 B.C. to 4 B.C., the latter date frequently offered by Bible scholars as the year of Christ's birth.

The Gospels declared the birth, life, death, and resurrection of the real King of the Jews. As the Book of Acts opens, Luke wants to record the history of how the King's people continue to proclaim His message during the first century after His death. Truly, the "Acts of the Apostles" are in reality, the Acts of Jesus Christ lived out through His followers. In these twelve studies, you will explore the many ways in which God used ordinary people to accomplish extraordinary ministry.

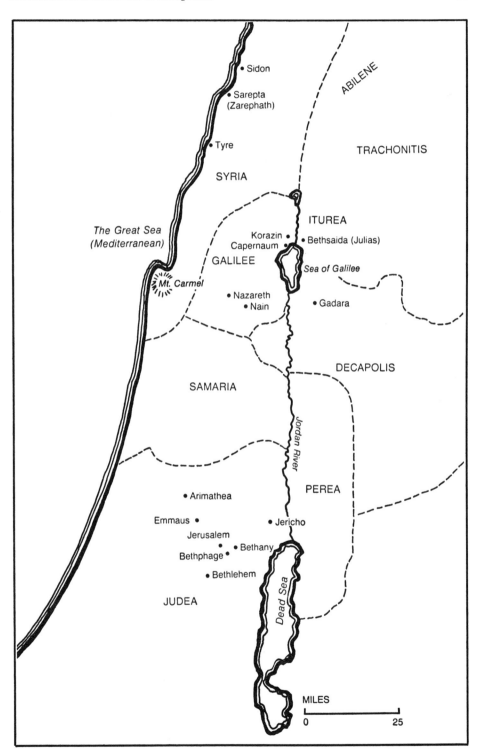

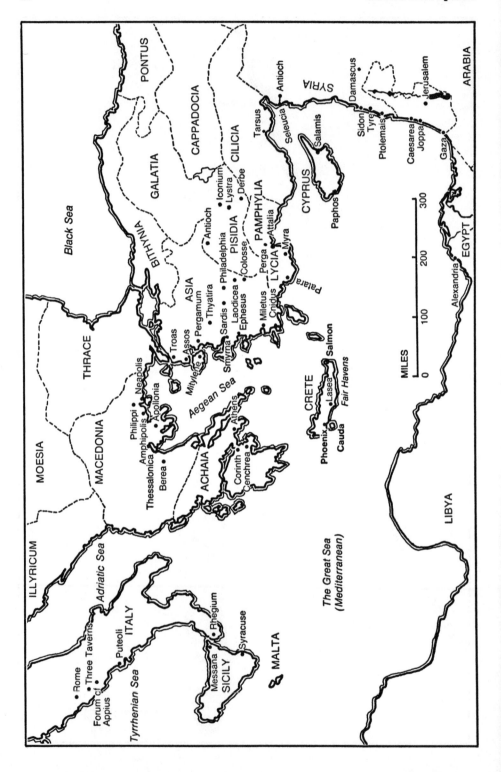

Acts 1:1-11

We Are Witnesses

In 1903, Bolshevism was born with seventeen supporters. By the mid-1980s, Communism controlled over 1 billion people, almost one fourth the population of the entire world. American Communists, not a dominant force on the political scene in the United States, reportedly contribute 38 percent of their gross annual income for the cause of Communism. American Christians, by contrast, give less than 1 percent.

It is almost as if the task of witnessing a message to the world were given by God to Communists rather than Christians. Yet the central theme of the Book of Acts focuses on that single dynamic word—*witnesses*. It appears thirty-nine times throughout the book and nowhere more prominently than in the eighth verse of chapter one—the key verse for the entire book.

Luke and Acts together make up approximately 30 percent of the entire New Testament. They were written to the same person—a Greek Christian named Theophilus—by the same person—Luke. They both cover about thirty-three years of time, and the papyrus rolls of the original manuscripts were probably almost equal in length.

The author, a medical doctor by profession and historian by avocation, is the only Gentile to author a New Testament book. His friend, Theophilus, may very well have been a professional peer, a man brilliant in intellect, diversified in interests, and highly professional in his lifestyle.

Acts was written somewhere in the early A.D. 60s, possibly from Caesarea or Rome. What we find in this book is a growing group of people who are genuinely excited about the resurrection of Jesus Christ and the coming of the Holy Spirit, and are thoroughly prepared to accept and activate the motto, "We are witnesses."

A. WITNESSES OF THE LORD'S LIFE *(Acts 1:1-5).*   Luke's essay opens with a paragraph describing the appearances of the Lord Jesus immediately following His resurrection. We can immediately see that the author intends this book to follow directly in line with his Gospel. The resemblance, for example, between Acts 1:4 and Luke 24:49 shows deliberate effort on the author's part to tie the two books together.

Examining the Text	*Explaining the Text*
1. Read Acts 1:1-5. Assuming Luke used the same approach to his writing of the Book of Acts as he did in his Gospel, compare Acts 1:1-5 with Luke 1:1-4. What are the characteristics of Luke's style of research and writing?	
2. The gift for which the disciples are asked to wait (v. 4) was the Holy Spirit. On the basis of what you know about the Gospels, why do you think Jesus asked them to wait in Jerusalem?	2. The phrase "kingdom of God" is commonly used in Acts to summarize the general Christian proclamation of the Gospel (8:12; 19:8; 20:25; 28:23, 31).
3. Study Matthew 3:11; Mark 1:8; and Acts 11:16. From what you read in these verses, what would you say is the difference between baptism with water and baptism with the Holy Spirit?	3. The word *baptism,* commonly associated with being "dipped or immersed" here seems to take on the significance of "joining" or "union."

B. WITNESSES OF THE LORD'S MESSAGE *(Acts 1:6-8).*   The idea of "the kingdom" still looms large in the minds of the disciples. But once again, the Lord rebukes their worldly thinking and tells them in unmistakable terms that the message of the kingdom is a message for the world. And the commission of the disciples becomes the theme of the church—to witness of Jesus Christ.

Explaining the Text

1. The issue at stake for the disciples was not the time of the kingdom's coming, but their present world around them.

2. Some commentators suggest that Acts 1:8 is not only the key verse of the book, but also a clue as to its organization—namely that witness to Jerusalem takes place in Acts 2:42–8:3; witness to Judea and Samaria is described in Acts 8:4–12:24; and witness to the world in Acts 12:25–28:31.

3. The word *witness* is a translation of the word from which we get our English word *martyr.*

Examining the Text

1. Read Acts 1:6-8. Compare Acts 1:6-8 with Matthew 13. What concern do the disciples express to Jesus? (v. 6) How do you explain their single-mindedness?

2. Locate on the map on page 11, the three geographical points to which Jesus refers (v. 8).

3. What is the significance of Jesus' choice of the word *witnesses* in verse 8? Write a few words describing the difference between their style of witness as recorded in the Gospels and what you already know about their ministry in the Book of Acts.

C. WITNESSES OF THE LORD'S ASCENSION (*Acts 1:9-11*).   Luke wastes no time in getting right into the flow of the text, rehearsing the events of the Resurrection, coming of the Holy Spirit, the Ascension, and anticipation of the Lord's return. In these brief verses we learn how important the Ascension is to the foundational doctrines throughout the Book of Acts and to the activity of the early Christians.

Examining the Text	Explaining the Text
1. Read Acts 1:9-11. Identify two phrases in these verses which suggest two major doctrines of the Christian faith (vv. 9 and 11).	1. The words *"looking intently"* describe the stunned response of the disciples to the Ascension. These words are used fourteen times in the New Testament, twelve of which are from the pen of Luke.
2. What three verbs does Luke use to describe the Lord's ascension? (vv. 9-11)	
3. Presumably, the "two men dressed in white" were angels. What is the significance of angelic messengers on this occasion?	3. The Ascension brought Christ's earthly ministry to a close and marked His exaltation to the right hand of the Father (Acts 2:33-36; 5:30-31; Hebrews 1:3; 8:1; 12:2).

Experiencing the Text

1. Note Luke's emphasis on "many convincing proofs" (v. 3). What are some of the proofs of our Lord's resurrection and how do they relate to your life and witness today?

2. The Book of Acts begins at Jerusalem, the major *city* of the nation of Israel. Numerous other *cities* are mentioned throughout the Book of Acts. List some of the implications of this for us today as it concerns evangelism.

Experiencing the Text

3. Verse 7 seems to refer to more than just the restoration of the kingdom, since the Lord uses a double plural—"times or dates." Give some examples of how you have struggled with God's timing, and the lessons He has taught you concerning His total control over both *what* happens in your life, as well as when it happens.

4. Some have suggested that Christians in countries where the church has not been persecuted tend to be careless about expecting Jesus' return. Assume for the moment they are right. How can you, as an individual Christian, retain a dynamic awareness that the Lord is coming back again?

Acts 1:12–2:47

Beginnings of the Church

At the end of the last lesson, we left the bewildered disciples standing looking into the sky as the Lord Jesus went back to the Father. Angels came to affirm the promise of His second coming, and Luke records that the eleven "returned to Jerusalem from the hill called the Mount of Olives." Jerusalem is the place of beginnings in the Book of Acts because it is the site of the Crucifixion, Resurrection, and the founding of the first New Testament church. In the passage before us, we learn how to choose church leaders, how to understand the importance of Pentecost and the Holy Spirit, and how to be the Church. There were just ten days between the Ascension and Pentecost, but they were enormously important days for those early believers.

A. SPIRITUAL PROCEDURES *(Acts 1:12-26).* Herschel Hobbs writes of Jesus' disciples, "The outstanding thing about these men is that they were not outstanding... [they were] ordinary men chosen to do an extraordinary task." God still works through ordinary people, and in this first section of our text for this lesson, we learn how to select church leaders using "spiritual procedures."

Examining the Text	*Explaining the Text*
1. Read Acts 1:12-26. Note the people involved in the disciples' list in verses 13-14 and compare it with Luke's list in Luke 6:12-16.	
2. What other believers are named in this early group? Where did they meet? What did they do there?	2. This passage contains the last mention of Mary the mother of Jesus in the New Testament (v. 14), and the reference to His half brothers corresponds with Luke's record in His Gospel (Luke 8:2-3; 23:49). Remember that the 120 believers in Jerusalem were not the only Christians in the country at this time; others would have been in Samaria and Galilee.
3. What were the qualifications for the new apostle? (vv. 21-22)	
4. How was the new apostle finally chosen (vv. 23-26) and what implications might the process have for such choices in our day?	4. Twelve is very important in Jewish symbolism (12 thrones [Matt. 19:28]; 12 foundations [Rev. 21:14]). The selection of Matthias emphasizes again that the church belongs to the Lord and not to us. This is the last time lots (very similar to dice) appear in the New Testament.

B. SPIRITUAL POWER *(Acts 2:1-21).* Pentecost, commonly known as the Feast of Weeks, was established fifteen centuries before Christ and became one of the three great pilgrim festivals of the Jews. The name was derived from the fact that it was celebrated the fiftieth day after Passover. In the Old Testament, it was viewed as the anniversary of the Law given at Sinai. Now under the New Covenant, it becomes the birthday of the Church.

Explaining the Text	*Examining the Text*
1. Fire is a common form of God's presence seen in the Old Testament (e.g., Moses and the burning bush [Ex. 3], and the fiery cloud at night that led the Israelites through the desert [Ex. 13:17-22]).	1. Read Acts 2:1-21. Name three audiovisual signs of the Spirit's coming (vv. 1-4).
	2. What caused the crowd to gather? (vv. 5-6)
	3. How did people respond to these signs?
	4. What is the significance of the way this section of our chapter ends—"And everyone who calls on the name of the Lord will be saved"? (v. 21)

C. SPIRITUAL PREACHING *(Acts 2:22-41).* There are twenty-three sermons or speeches recorded in the Book of Acts and seven of them are delivered by the Apostle Peter. In this section of verses he emphasizes that the messiahship of Jesus will be the church's witness to the Jews and that God has affirmed Jesus' ministry through the Resurrection.

Examining the Text

1. Read Acts 2:22-41. According to Peter, how did God work out His purpose in the life and ministry of Jesus?

2. Why is the Resurrection so important to the Gospel?

3. In verse 36, Peter says, "God has made this Jesus, whom you crucified, both Lord and Christ." What do you understand to be the difference in those terms?

4. How does Peter get his hearers to see their need of salvation?

5. Why is repentance an important part of the Gospel message?

Explaining the Text

1. The inclusion of Psalm 16:8-11 is important. It shows that Messiah's death was God's will. This psalm emphasizes God's sovereignty and offers praise for His control of the universe.

4. Christ is the key to the Scriptures and the unifying thread between the Old Testament and the New Testament.

5. The word *repent* in verse 38 is the Greek word *metaneo*, which means "turn and go the other way."

D. SPIRITUAL PEOPLE *(Acts 2:42-47)*.   During the Day of Pentecost, about 3,000 people were added to the initial number of 120 believers in Jerusalem. Then the real work began. What did these people do when they gathered together? How did the apostles interpret all that Jesus had taught them during the three-and-a-half years they had spent with Him—especially the last forty days, between the Resurrection and Ascension? What does it mean today to be spiritual people of God?

Explaining the Text

1. This passage emphasizes the church in three dimensions—worship, work, and witness.

3. In the early chapters of Acts, good Christians were still good Jews, so temple worship was very much in order. These new converts also needed to know doctrine, so teaching was crucial. This early church was also characterized as a joyful people—which did not go unnoticed by Luke. (The word *praising* [*ainountes*] is used only nine times in the NT, seven of them by Luke: Luke 2:13, 20; 19:37; 24:53; Acts 2:47; 3:8-9; Rom. 15:11; Rev. 19:5.)

Examining the Text

1. Read Acts 2:42-47. In what ways were these Christians different from people around them? (vv. 42-45)

2. What characteristics marked their public worship? (vv. 46-47)

3. One might say that the early church grew "from the inside out." What do you think this statement means in light of what we read in this passage? (vv. 42-47)

Experiencing the Text

1. In a brief paragraph, state the biblical qualifications you consider important for church leaders today and how congregations can choose their officers wisely.

Experiencing the Text

2. Do you agree or disagree with this statement: "The power of Pentecost is primarily a person"? Explain.

3. You may never preach to thousands in a major city, but you can still witness your faith in Christ to others you meet. In the space provided below, write five crucial truths of the Gospel which you think should be included when sharing Christ with someone else. Then suggest a Bible reference which supports each truth.

  Gospel Truth   *Supporting Passage*

 1.

 2.

 3.

 4.

 5.

4. If your church is like most others, there are some ways in which it is *like* the church in Jerusalem and other ways in which it is different. In the three sections which follow, write down the ways you think your church is similar, how it is different, and some of the changes you think might make your church more biblical.

Ways in Which Our Church Exhibits Biblical Characteristics

Ways in Which Our Church Falls Short of These Characteristics

Ways in Which Our Church Can Become More Biblical

Acts 3–5

Early Ministry in Jerusalem

In September 1900, the most devastating hurricane in American history came ashore with blinding force, hitting the island city of Galveston, Texas. Though early detection and alarm systems were not as sophisticated then as they are now, residents of the island were given ample warning, alerting them to the danger of the impending storm. Only one old bridge connected Galveston Island with the mainland, and evacuation had to be swift and immediate. We are told that people went out to the shore, looked out across the Gulf of Mexico, but saw no signs of disturbance. Many shrugged their shoulders, complained of being bothered by civil authorities, and returned to their homes. The hurricane hit. Six thousand people were killed and the city was destroyed—a tragedy which could have been averted, had people only listened to the warning.

In his essay to Theophilus, Luke has already issued one such warning, recorded at the end of Peter's pentecostal sermon in Jerusalem (Acts 2:36-41). Several more warnings follow as the word begins to spread around the city and the exemplary lifestyle of the early Christians hits the hypocritical world of first-century Judaism like the hurricane of 1900 hit Galveston. Acts 3 records an impromptu message on the name of Jesus, delivered by Peter just outside the temple. Then in chapter 4 we find Peter's defense before the Sanhedrin with its ringing declaration, "Salvation is found in no one else for there is no other name under heaven given to men by which we must be saved" (Acts 4:12). In Acts 5, God shows us how serious He is about the purity of the church when Ananias and Sapphira are struck dead for lying to the Holy Spirit. Witnesses? Yes, these early Christians were witnesses at every possible opportunity. Warned? Anyone who listened heard plainly the message of the Gospel in his own language and with allusions to his own culture and history. The Good News had been unleashed and Jerusalem would never be the same again.

A. MINISTRY AT THE TEMPLE *(Acts 3:1-26).*   Fervent Jews in Jesus' day met at the temple three times a day for prayer—during morning sacrifice, during the afternoon sacrifice, and at sunset. In chapter 3 of Acts, Peter and John are not looking for ministry opportunities, but are simply "going to church" as was their normal pattern.

Examining the Text	*Explaining the Text*
1. Read Acts 3:1-26. In the first seven verses of this chapter, we see a notable change in the behavior of Peter and John (cf. Mark 14:47, 66-71; John 18:10-11). How do you account for the difference in their behavior on this occasion?	1. Almsgiving was a meritorious act among devout Jews in the first century. Therefore, a seat just outside the temple gate was a good location for a lame beggar.
2. In your own words, describe the people's reaction to this miracle.	
3. Some people today would say that this kind of physical healing is available for all Christians and need only be claimed. Do you agree or disagree? Explain why.	
4. Undoubtedly, there were hundreds of beggars around Jerusalem. How do you explain God's focusing on this one man?	
5. Can you identify five names (titles) Peter used in this passage to describe Jesus? Why do you think he focused so quickly on the *name* of Jesus, rather than on some other aspect of Christian doctrine? *Names* *Verses*	5. Customarily, Jewish names were not for identity purposes alone. A name was also intended to express the nature of the person's being. In this brilliant impromptu sermon on the temple porch, Peter deals with five different names/titles for Jesus.

B. MINISTRY BEFORE THE SANHEDRIN *(Acts 4:1-22)*. Early Jewish opposition came mainly from the Sadducees who were priests from the tribe of Levi. As such, they were fanatical about protecting Jewish tradition. In this passage, Luke portrays them as being deeply disturbed because the teaching of the apostles—especially this business about Jesus having been raised from the dead—was upsetting the *status quo* of the city. In spite of imprisonment, the Gospel continues to claim followers, and the dominant theme of Peter's preaching focuses on the power and authority of the name of Jesus.

Explaining the Text

1. The Sanhedrin, which served somewhat as a Supreme Court and Senate of the nation, consisted of three groups—the rulers (high priests), elders, and teachers of the Law (scribes). Together they numbered seventy-one (the high priest plus seventy others).

Examining the Text

1. Read Acts 4:1-22. Why were Peter and John brought before the Sanhedrin on this particular occasion? (v. 2)

2. Throughout the Book of Acts, the Sanhedrin seems to consistently oppose the Gospel. Why do you think they did this?

3. The central issue of discussion continues to be the name of Jesus Christ, and is brought up at least four times in our passage (vv. 10, 12, 17, and 18). The Sanhedrin couldn't deny the miracle Peter and John had performed. Surely it was obvious to them that Jesus Christ was central in the lives and preaching of the members of the early church.

3. When asked about the healing of the lame man, Peter could have simply said, "God did it" and probably would have been released on the spot. But he doesn't. Why do you think he makes such a fuss over the name of Jesus? (vv. 8-12)

Examining the Text

Explaining the Text

4. Why were the rulers and elders of the people surprised by what John and Peter said and did? (vv. 13-17)

5. How does God use ordinary men and women in extraordinary ways today?

6. The question of civil disobedience stands squarely in our path as we look at Acts 4:18-20. Under what conditions, if any, is it biblical for Christians to disobey government today? (You may want to review Romans 13 and 1 Peter 2.)

C. MINISTRY THROUGH PRAYER AND SHARING *(Acts 4:23-37)*. What were the first Christians really like? Luke wants Theophilus to know so he describes them in two ways. First of all, they were people who prayed together (vv. 23-31) and second, they were people who shared what they had with those who had need (vv. 32-37).

Examining the Text

Explaining the Text

1. Read Acts 4:23-37. Notice how the prayer of these early believers begins—"Sovereign Lord" (v. 24). Why would these Christians begin their prayer by emphasizing God's sovereignty?

1. The foundation for the prayer of the church is the sovereignty of God. The term they use is *despotes* which appears ten times in New Testament prayers. Note also the unity of the church—"they raised their voices together" (v. 24).

Explaining the Text	*Examining the Text*
	2. Consider the nature of this prayer. It was not a prayer of thanksgiving for the release of Peter and John. Nor was it a petition for relief from further persecution by the Sanhedrin. Why, then, do you think these Christians prayed as they did? (vv. 24-30)
	3. How do you explain verse 32, which states, "No one claimed that any of his possessions was his own, but they shared everything they had"? What would you say to someone who says this verse advocates a form of Communism?
	4. List several characteristics of these early Christians you would like to be evident in your own life and in the lives of members in your church (vv. 32-35).
5. Barnabas' real name was Joseph. The apostles had nicknamed him Barnabas, which means "son of encouragement."	5. In verse 36, Luke introduces Barnabas. What reason would he have for introducing Barnabas so briefly at this point? How does he exemplify the believers in the early church at Jerusalem?

D. MINISTRY IN SPITE OF DEATH AND DISGRACE *(Acts 5:1-42).* Just about the time it seems safe to declare the church's unprecedented success, in walk Ananias and Sapphira. Luke seems to contrast their greed with the generosity of Barnabas, described at the end of chapter 4. The Bible tells the story exactly as it happened. It was a vignette of warning to the early believers in Jerusalem as it is for Christians everywhere today.

Examining the Text

1. Read Acts 5:1-42. Then go back and take a more analytical look at verses 1-11. What sin did Ananias and Sapphira actually commit? (vv. 3-4)

2. What factors do you think may have prompted Ananias and Sapphira to carry out their plan?

3. Notice how Luke follows the account of Ananias and Sapphira with a more positive paragraph, which is filled with miracles (vv. 12-16). Why do you think Luke did that?

4. Follow carefully the events described in verses 17-33 of Acts 5. What was there about the sequence of activities that would have brought forth such fury and anger from the members of the Sanhedrin?

5. Based on what you read about Gamaliel in this chapter (vv. 34-40), what sort of person do you think he may have been?

Explaining the Text

1. This account in Scripture is reminiscent of the story of Achan in Joshua 7 (cf. Num. 15:32-36; 16:1-35).

3. The paragraph, beginning at verse 12, shows reason for the Sadducees' jealousy—the apostles had broken the "No Witnessing" law.

4. Enter the Pharisees, and particularly, the brilliant Gamaliel. Standing in the line of the great Hillel, he was surely the most respected member of the Sanhedrin. His appeal for reason reminds us of two other Pharisees, introduced in the Gospels—Nicodemus and Joseph of Arimathea.

Experiencing the Text

1. In what ways has God "surprised" you with ministry opportunities? List two or three things He has brought your way over the past six months which were unexpected, but joyous events of service.

2. In Acts 3:11-16, Peter denied taking any personal responsibility for the miracle he performed. Rather he emphasized the name of Jesus, a phrase Luke uses thirty-three times in the Book of Acts. In what ways has the name and work of Jesus punctuated your own witness?

3. What valuable prayer principles can you find in Acts 4:23-31? How would you like to see these principles transform your prayer life?

4. Reread Acts 5:40-42. In what ways have you been "counted worthy of suffering disgrace for the name [of Jesus]"? Be specific.

Acts 6–7

Stephen and the Six Servants

In *The House of the Dead*, Dostoyevski described work which had "the character of complete uselessness" as the worst possible punishment. "A prisoner consigned to a repetitive, valueless task," he said, would "strangle himself or commit a thousand crimes punishable with death, rather than live in such an abject condition and endure such torments."

Though this Russian novelist may have overstated the case a bit, uselessness remains the dread fate of thousands who retire or who, for some reason, lose their jobs each year. But uselessness was hardly a problem in the early church. In Acts 6–7, Luke described a growing church whose organizational problems were the result of rapid expansion. The first five chapters of Acts have been all-Jerusalem and all-Jewish. In chapters 6–9, Luke shifts his focus to Stephen, Philip, and Saul, while the cultural and ethnic scenario favors Samaria and the Greeks. Imagine how Theophilus must have perked up as he began reading the story of "Stephen and the Six Servants."

As you study Acts 6–7, remember that, like Barnabas in chapter 5, all these men are laymen. It's difficult to think of the apostles as laymen, since they spent three-and-a-half years in "seminary," with the Lord Jesus as their only professor. Apart from Paul, virtually everyone we meet in the Book of Acts is a lay leader in the early church. What this passage said to those who served Christ in the church of the first century, it also says to us about serving Christ in the church of the twentieth century!

A. NEED AND QUALITIES OF A BIBLICAL SERVANT *(Acts 6:1-4)*.   The "Grecian Jews" mentioned in this passage had lived most of their lives outside of Palestine. Their primary language was Greek rather than Aramaic, and their culture "foreign" by Palestinian standards. The distrust which "home country" Jews held for these people may explain the problem which surfaces in this chapter.

Examining the Text	*Explaining the Text*
1. Read Acts 6:1-4. Note the process of selection used to choose the church's first deacons. In sequential order, list the steps the apostles took to handle the situation described in 6:1.	1. The word *disciples,* used twice in this paragraph, appears for the first time here in Acts. Isn't it interesting that both factions are called "disciples"?
2. What reasons do you think the apostles may have had for delegating this problem to other people, rather than handling it themselves?	
3. How did these early Christians know whom to choose? What specific spiritual qualities were they looking for? (v. 3)	
4. Why do you suppose these particular qualities were chosen?	

B. CHOICE AND CHALLENGE OF A BIBLICAL SERVANT *(Acts 6:5-15)*. The apostles made the proposal and set down guidelines, but the church made the decision. This is an excellent example of participative leadership among the believers in the early church. All seven servants chosen had Greek names and may well have been Grecian Jews themselves.

Explaining the Text	*Examining the Text*
1. The "seven servants" described in verses 1-6 are frequently referred to as "deacons," though they are not actually called that in the text. They did function, however, according to Paul's description of a deacon in 1 Timothy 3:8-13.	1. Read Acts 6:5-15. Notice that Stephen had additional qualifications, not mentioned of the others (v. 5). Why do you think Luke made a point of mentioning those qualities?
	2. In this passage, we see that the qualities which characterized God's servants were beginning to increase. Compare verses 3, 5, and 8 of Acts 6 and note the development of ministerial qualities. How do these qualities compare?
	3. Note the effects of this wise selection of good men. Beginning with verse 7, and studying through to the end of the chapter, list several things that happened as the result of their appointment.
	4. Think back to the Gospel accounts of the trial of Jesus (cf. Matt. 26:57-68; Mark 14:53–15:20; Luke 22:66 –23:23; John 18:28–19:16). In what ways were the trial of Jesus and the trial of Stephen similar?

C. MATURITY AND GIFTS OF A BIBLICAL SERVANT *(Acts 7:1-50)*. Stephen's speech to the Sanhedrin can be divided into five basic parts: Abraham and the land (7:2-8); Joseph in Egypt (7:9-16); Moses and deliverance (7:17-36); Israel and rejection (7:37-43) and God and the temple (7:44-50). It is a brilliant proclamation of the Christian message in terms of popular first-century Judaism and it focuses directly on the three pillars of Israel before the Roman destruction in A.D. 70—the land, the Law, and the temple.

Examining the Text	*Explaining the Text*
1. Read Acts 7:1-50. How would you describe Stephen's approach in answering the charges leveled against him? Why do you think he chose this approach?	1. Stephen offers the Sanhedrin not a scholarly historical survey (which is what this chapter may look like to us), but rather, a theological explanation of God's dealings with Israel. He shows that God's blessing is not inseparably linked with the land, with Moses, or with any particular geographical location.
2. How does Stephen's long explanation of Old Testament history prepare his hearers to respond to the message of the Gospel?	2. Today we refer to Stephen's approach as "preevangelism," a technique also used by Peter in chapter 2 of Acts. The intent of preevangelism is to give people who do not understand the Gospel enough background to make sense of what they hear.
3. Why do you think Stephen ends his speech by focusing on the tabernacle and the temple? (vv. 44-50) Compare this passage with Jesus' words in John 4:21-24.	

D. COURAGE AND GRACE OF A BIBLICAL SERVANT *(Acts 7:51-60).* Suddenly Stephen sets an entirely new tone in Christian preaching. His use of the word *our* switches to *you.* And from the viewpoint of the Sanhedrin, this gracious and courageous lay leader is guilty of flagrant apostasy—especially if he is a Hellenist. The result? His immediate death by stoning. And Stephen becomes the first martyr of the New Testament church.

Explaining the Text	*Examining the Text*
	1. Read Acts 7:51-60. Notice how the tone of Stephen's message changes in verse 51. What charges did Stephen make against the religious leaders of his day? (vv. 51-53)
	Why do you suppose he spoke to the people as he did?
2. The identification of God, heaven, and Jesus in our passage again affirms the deity of Christ. The phrase, "Son of man," though used frequently in the Gospels, is used outside the Gospels only here and in Revelation 1:13 and 14:14.	2. In verses 54-58, we see several evidences of out-of-control anger. Find and name them.
3. The word *asleep* in verse 60 is a verb form from which we construct the English noun "cemetery." A cemetery—supposedly fearsome and spooky—is a Christian word of faith. Christians who die are not gone; they are temporarily asleep.	3. The euphemism of "sleep" for death is not unusual in the New Testament. (Remember Jesus' words about Lazarus in John 11?) Why do you suppose the early believers spoke of death in this way?
	4. In verses 54-60, we see an outstanding demonstration of godly character in the life of Stephen. List several things he said and did which marked him as a special servant of the Lord.

Experiencing the Text

1. Quickly review Acts 6:1-4. What can today's church learn from the apostles about how to handle problems in the church?

2. Choosing *qualified* men to serve in places of leadership was obviously very important to the early church. Do you think we have become lax in our standards for church leaders today? Why or why not?

3. Stephen was a remarkable lay leader in the early church. What can churches today do to help their lay leaders "produce" like Stephen did?

4. Can you think of anyone in your church who shows the characteristics demonstrated in Stephen's life? Write a brief paragraph about that person.

5. We in the so-called "free world" may not always enjoy the freedom we do now. What do you see in the life of Stephen that could better prepare you to face persecution?

Acts 8–9

Three People God Used

One story which has grown up around the life and work of Andrew Carnegie centers on his deep commitment to the quality of people who work for him. "Take away my people but leave my factories," he said, "and soon grass will grow up through the floors of the factories. But leave my people and take my factories, and those people will soon build new and better factories." Without question, the key ingredient in ministry, as well as in business, is the quality of the people. In this lesson, we will see Luke's "home movies" of three dedicated people in the early church who provide adventure and add color to the Book of Acts.

This passage is introduced by Luke's contrast between Stephen, who was martyred for his faith (7:59-60), and Saul, who zealously persecuted the early church (8:1). At first, this persecution must have seemed like some sort of horror story to those young believers, especially the Hellenistic Christians at whom the persecution seemed to be primarily directed. But then—as Luke reminds us—we see God's plan realized and in time the Gospel spreads from Jerusalem to Judea and Samaria.

All of us who are a part of Christ's body, the church, are greatly interested in the vast differences among Christians. The original twelve disciples were unlike one another, though they had certain occupational and personality traits in common. In Acts 8–9 we find three people who come from totally different backgrounds: Philip, the Hellenistic lay evangelist; Saul, the brilliant and cruel Pharisee; and a simple woman named Dorcas, the only female in the New Testament to whom the term "disciple" is specifically and personally applied.

This "bringing together" of vastly different people into one body is the genius of Christian unity. Paul lauded it in the early verses of Ephesians 4, while to the Romans he wrote, "Just as each of us has one body with many members, and these members do not all have the same function, so in Christ we who are many form one body, and each member belongs to all the others" (Rom. 12:4-5).

A. PHILIP: DEACON IN ACTION *(Acts 8:1-40).* One of the seven lay leaders elected in chapter 6 of Acts, this Philip should not be confused with the apostle, Philip, whose name appears frequently in the Gospels. Perhaps we can distinguish between them by calling the Philip of our present study, "The Evangelist," for that is precisely what he was.

Examining the Text	*Explaining the Text*
1. Read Acts 8:1-40. Then, using a Bible dictionary or encyclopedia, find out everything you can about Philip. Where else is he mentioned in the New Testament?	
2. How would you describe the "faith" of Simon the Sorcerer? (vv. 9-13, 18-23)	
3. When the Bible uses the term "believe," it does not always describe people who are saved. That may be the case with Simon, and was certainly true of the people described at the end of John 2. What, then, is *saving faith?* How would you define it?	
4. Why did Peter and John come down from Jerusalem when they heard "that Samaria had accepted the Word of God"? (vv. 14-17)	4. The visible sign accompanying the coming of the Holy Spirit here (vv. 15-17) might well have been speaking of tongues, though Scripture does not say so (cf. 2:4). Perhaps God wanted to preserve the unity of the church—a tough task when dealing with Jerusalem and Samaria.

Explaining the Text	Examining the Text
5. Gaza was the southern-most of five chief Philistine cities. It was located about 50 miles southwest of Jerusalem. The eunuch mentioned in this passage was doubtless a "prose-lyte of the gate," a term used of foreigners who accept-ed the Law and the Jewish religion.	5. In verse 35, we read, "Then Philip began with that very passage of Scripture [Isa. 53:7-8] and told him the good news about Jesus." Make a list of some of the things Philip might have told the eunuch.

B. SAUL: GOD'S CHOSEN INSTRUMENT *(Acts 9:1-31).*   Cunning and crafty, this young rabbi from Tarsus was a zealot in his goal to exterminate Christians. He was not content to let his persecution of the church end with the death of Stephen and the expulsion of believers from Jerusalem. Instead, Saul obtained permission from the high priest and headed north to Damascus, in Syria, with the intent of bringing back prisoner any Christians he might find. A light from heaven, the call of Ananias, blindness and physical healing, and the ministry in Damascus are well-known highlights of the Book of Acts for most Christians.

Explaining the Text	Examining the Text
1. Up to this point, the believers were not yet called "Christians." Saul calls them followers of "the Way," a phrase which appears numerous other times in the Book of Acts (19:9, 23; 22:4; 24:14, 22).	1. Read Acts 9:1-31. Write a biographical sketch of Saul. Compare Acts 8:1-3 with Acts 9:1-9, 17-22.

2. With the conversion of Saul, we see the strategy of evangelism changing. In what ways and why is it changing? |

Examining the Text	*Explaining the Text*
3. Shortly after his conversion, Saul became a "basket case" in his escape from Damascus (9:23-25). Who were the "followers" who lowered him to safety in a basket through an opening in the wall?	3. Luke's account of Saul's early ministry is offered in brief, partly because of his unique purpose in writing to Theophilus but also because he anticipated that the believers would read Paul's account in Galatians 1:15-24.
4. How do you explain the great faith Barnabas showed in Saul (9:26-27) when no one else was willing to believe he was really Christ's disciple? What characteristics of this man's life are portrayed in Acts 9?	4. Partly for his own protection, and partly because they didn't want another incident to take place like the one with Stephen, the apostles sent Saul back to Tarsus. It is possible that the hardships which Paul records in 2 Corinthians 11:23-27 occurred during this period of his life.

C. DORCAS: DOER OF GOOD DEEDS *(Acts 9:32-43)*. Thirty-five miles northwest of Jerusalem lies the only natural harbor between Egypt and Ptolemais. Today it is called Haifa. In New Testament times it was called Joppa—home of Dorcas, Mrs. Ordinary Christian. Here is a simple lady around whom no excitement flurries. Her entire life may have been spent in and around one town; it is likely she was unknown beyond Joppa's city limits. Yet in twelve short verses, Luke shows us, through Dorcas, how to exercise the gift of helps, how to serve the Lord while single, and how to die like a Christian.

Examining the Text	*Explaining the Text*
1. Locate Lydda and Joppa on the map on page 12. Note their location in relationship to Jerusalem.	1. Tel Aviv-Jaffa is the largest city in modern-day Israel. This ancient seaport, located just 10 miles beyond Lydda, dates back to Old Testament times (Josh. 19:46; Jonah 1:3).

Explaining the Text

2. The gift of helps is mentioned in Romans 12:7 (serving) and 1 Corinthians 12:28 and seems to describe the manner in which God enables certain Christians to take the burdens of others upon themselves.

Examining the Text

2. Why do you think Luke included this account about Dorcas in his history of the early church?

Why do you think he chose to put it at this point in the book?

3. During Peter's travels, he finds believers in Lydda and Joppa. How had these people heard the Gospel? Suggest several possible answers.

4. Peter stayed with a tanner named Simon who was considered unclean by the rabbis. Can you explain why Peter seemed less than zealous in maintaining strict Jewish ritual?

Experiencing the Text

1. The life of Simon the Sorcerer helps us see why it is important to know how to discern truth from error. In a world which is so full of confused and cultic beliefs, how can we learn to discern truth from error?

2. What are two or three specific things you learned about personal evangelism from Philip's experience with the Ethiopian eunuch? (Focus on Philip's technique and message in sharing the Gospel.)

Experiencing the Text

3. From the account of Saul's conversion we learn some dramatic lessons about the will of God. When you and/or members of your family have major decisions to make (i.e., possibility of moving, job change, choice of college, etc.), how do you arrive at what you believe to be God's will?

4. In the conversion experience of Saul, we see the amazing grace of our Lord demonstrated—anyone can be saved, even a persecuting Pharisee. How would you define *grace?* How is God's grace seen in salvation? And how have you seen God's grace demonstrated in your daily life?

5. Dorcas is a wonderful example of the oft-repeated scriptural injunction, "Remember widows, orphans, and strangers." In what ways do you acknowledge and act on this biblical principle?

6. We don't know that Dorcas had no husband, though, of course, he is not mentioned in this passage (Acts 9:36-39). She, herself, may have been a widow. Ministry to singles of all ages has become an important component in our twentieth-century churches. Name some ways in which your church either *is* ministering to singles or could do so more effectively.

7. The death of Dorcas offers us an example of how a Christian can meet death with dignity. Though her death was not at all dramatic, like the death of Stephen, Dorcas died like a Christian. How would you explain what it means to "die like a Christian"? How are our churches helping people today learn to do this?

Acts 10–12

Apostolic Adventures

Up to this point in the Book of Acts, all the Christian converts have been Jews from the land of Palestine or those dispersed around the Mediterranean world who have come back to Palestine for the Passover, Pentecost, or for some other reason. But in Acts 10, all that changes as a Roman soldier by the name of Cornelius trusts Christ. The early church resisted Gentiles being accepted or even evangelized (10:14, 28; 11:2-3, 8). But in these three chapters we see God Himself introducing Gentiles into the church.

Interestingly enough, it is Peter, not Paul, who is the human instrument God uses to reach Cornelius with the Gospel. A recent convert to Christianity, Paul—formerly Saul of Tarsus—later becomes the "apostle to the Gentiles." But for now, it is Peter who is sent with the Gospel to the Gentiles. Besides Cornelius and Peter, Barnabas and Herod Agrippa I—that ancient example of corrupt government—are included in the apostolic adventures included in this study.

The central theme we see running through Acts 10–12 is that "God does not show favoritism" (10:34). This is rather a foreign idea to these early Christians, particularly as Peter explains that Jehovah is now going to accept people "from every nation who fear Him and do what is right." The theology of the remnant, so common in Old Testament prophecy, now becomes a major component of the New Testament Gospel.

A. CORNELIUS—JEHOVAH'S CENTURION *(Acts 10:1-48)*.   The action in this account takes place at Caesarea, which was located 65 miles northwest of Jerusalem. This city was named in honor of Augustus, and in New Testament times, it was the Roman capital of the province of Judea. Cornelius is the outstanding example in Scripture of how God honors a person's willingness to follow what light he has by giving him more light, which in this case was the light of the Gospel.

Examining the Text	*Explaining the Text*
1. Read Acts 10:1-48. Write a brief character sketch of Cornelius.	1. A centurion was a non-commissioned officer who had worked his way up through the ranks, somewhat equal to a captain in today's military status. He commanded a regiment, one tenth of a legion, probably somewhere between 300-600 men.
Why do you think this account of Cornelius occupies so much space in the Book of Acts.	
2. Suppose you really believed God wanted you to do something that violated all the principles you had stood for throughout your life. Would you do it? Why?	2. The word for hungry (*prospeinos*) only appears here in the New Testament (10:10) and is meant to convey a special God-ordained hunger. Peter's response reminds us of the words in Ezekiel 4:14.
How would you know whether or not it was really God who was prompting you to do this? How do you think Peter knew? (vv. 9-16)	
3. Verses 34-43 of Acts 10 might be considered the summary statements of Peter's sermon in Caesarea. What key elements did he include?	

Explaining the Text	*Examining the Text*
	How essential are these elements in sharing the Gospel today?
	4. Why is it important for us to demonstrate that "God does not show favoritism"?
	In what ways might we—the church—*not* be demonstrating this truth?

B. PETER—PORTRAIT IN HANDLING CRITICISM *(Acts 11:1-18).* Rejoicing in the excitement of the events at Caesarea, Peter returns to Jerusalem, perhaps expecting one, gigantic praise service. Instead, he runs into that standard quality which is found in abundance throughout the human species—criticism.

Explaining the Text	*Examining the Text*
1. Note that the criticism Peter received when he returned to Jerusalem came from "circumcised believers" who responded without having first heard the full story of what God had done.	1. Read Acts 11:1-18. What was the main criticism leveled against Peter by the apostles and "brothers" when he returned to Jerusalem? (v. 3)
	Why do you think they were more concerned about this than they were about his sharing the Gospel with a Gentile?
	2. Notice the new Peter here. How has he changed from his earlier days as a disciple described in the Gospels? (cf. Luke 9:18-33; 22:20-34, 47-62)

Examining the Text

3. Sometimes, those who criticize us don't understand our spiritual goals; they may be ignorant of our motives. According to Proverbs 15:1, how are we to handle this sort of criticism?

Consider the words of Jesus in Matthew 5:23-24; 7:1-5; and 18:15-17. How might Jesus' words have helped Peter react rightly when accused wrongly?

Explaining the Text

3. The momentous response of Cornelius and his household and the acceptance of the church in Jerusalem is encouraging. Yet these were hardly a solution to all the problems.

C. BARNABAS—FROM LAY LEADER TO PASTOR *(Acts 11:19-30)*. Is there a model church in the New Testament? Some would say the church at Ephesus because of plaudits described in the Book of Revelation. But the church at Antioch has got to be in the running, partly because of the splendid leadership of Barnabas (Son of Encouragement) and his teaching assistant, Saul of Tarsus. It was a church founded on aggressive evangelism, fortified by qualified leaders, fed by competent teachers, and functioning to meet the needs of others. That formula for an effective church is tough to beat!

Examining the Text

1. Read Acts 11:19-30. Notice how verse 19 picks up where Acts 8:4 left off—almost as if the scores of intervening verses had never been written. Also note Luke's mention of some new geographical locations, beginning in this section. Check the map on page 12 for the following locations: Phoenicia, Cyprus, Cyrene, Tarsus, and Antioch of Syria.

Explaining the Text

1. Antioch of Syria, founded about 300 B.C. and named for Antiochus the Great, lay 300 miles north of Jerusalem and 20 miles inland from the Mediterranean Sea. At the time of the founding of the church here, it was the third largest city in the Roman Empire (surpassed in size only by Rome and Alexandria). Antioch was a sprawling metropolis of some 500,000 people.

Explaining the Text	Examining the Text
	2. Once again we see a truly Christian character demonstrated in the life of Barnabas. How does Luke describe him here? (vv. 22-24)
	Why does Barnabas go to Tarsus? What risks may have been involved in doing this, and what does this indicate to us about Barnabas' leadership qualities?
	3. Tucked in amidst the rest of the story there is a brief but dramatic line, "The disciples were called Christians first at Antioch" (11:26). What does the term "Christian" mean to you?
	What do you think it meant to the folks at Antioch who first used the term?

D. HEROD—DON'T PUSH GOD TOO FAR *(Acts 12:1-24).* This chapter might well be titled, "The Adventures of a Prison Escapee." The year is A.D. 44; the season, spring. Here we are introduced to the first exhibition of church-state relations, and though the death of James certainly must have rocked the believers, we see that the people of God are the ultimate winners. Luke is careful to tell us the result of this tragedy: "The Word of God continued to increase and spread" (12:24). While Acts 12 opens by showing us a powerful king and a praying church, it closes by describing a dead king and a dynamic church.

Explaining the Text	Examining the Text
1. The Herod mentioned in Acts 12 was the grandson of Herod the Great.	1. Read Acts 12:1-24. In this passage, how do you explain the fact of James being put to death, while Peter is miraculously set free?

Examining the Text	Explaining the Text
How would you define the sovereignty of God in matters such as this?	
2. The church was praying "earnestly" for Peter's release, yet when he showed up at the door they could not believe he was standing there. How would you explain the church's apparent lack of faith on this occasion?	2. The Greek word translated "by itself" is *automate.* When God wants His servants in or out of a place, He opens the doors "automatically."
3. Study carefully the way Luke describes Herod's death in verses 21-23. Also notice the connecting word *but* used at the beginning of verse 24. What subtle but important point is Luke making in the text right here?	

Experiencing the Text

1. It is possible to be overscrupulous about some things, to the point of even going beyond God's Word and will. Can you think of an example demonstrating this sort of thing? Describe it.

2. Few lessons could be more practical for Christians in our day than to learn how to handle criticism in a biblical way. Describe a time when you were unjustly criticized. How *did* you respond? Based on Peter's example (11:4-17), how *should* you respond when you are unjustly criticized?

Experiencing the Text

3. The church at Antioch was founded by aggressive evangelism. What techniques of evangelism are currently being used in your church? Describe them and evaluate their effectiveness.

4. When Peter was in prison, the church prayed (12:5). In fact, that was their only available weapon (2 Cor. 10:4a). What kinds of battles have you fought using the weapon of prayer?

5. For what things have you prayed and yet not expected God to answer directly? How can you increase your ability to pray in faith, *believing* God?

Acts 13–15

The First Missionary Journey

Missiologist Ralph Winter has given his life to alerting Christians to the world's "hidden peoples." He and his staff indicate that though there are yet 17,000 mission fields, our globe contains some 2.5 million Bible-believing congregations and 150 congregations per mission field. Peter Wagner, writing in *Christianity Today*, suggests that as many as 78,000 people become Christians every day.

Yet even with all this progress, the need around the world continues to be acute. Over 2 billion people have no access whatsoever to the Gospel, and translation of the Scriptures into multitudinous languages is a task which still awaits our most careful and dedicated attention.

Bearing this in mind, let's go back and see how the early church sent out its first missionaries, how they ministered, and what kind of results they achieved. Acts 13 is a watershed chapter in the book and in the record of the New Testament. Here the spotlight shifts from Jerusalem to Antioch, from Peter to Paul, from the Jews to the Gentiles, and from Palestine to the entire Mediterranean world.

The year is about A.D. 48. And Luke's excitement seems to flow through his words as he describes how the Gospel is carried to the Gentiles on a full-scale basis. As you study, keep in mind that Luke himself was a Gentile and a traveling companion of the Apostle Paul during his second and third missionary journeys.

A. HOW TO SEND OUT MISSIONARIES *(Acts 13:1-12)*.   All the ingredients were right at Antioch—willing workers, a worshiping congregation, and wise procedures. Very likely this kind of bold missionary thrust could not have been accomplished in the much more conservative congregation at Jerusalem. In these twelve verses, we learn how to send out the people God chooses, to provide whatever they need, and to expect mixed results.

Examining the Text	*Explaining the Text*
1. Read Acts 13:1-12. Describe the activities of the early church which led to the sending out of the first missionaries (vv. 1-4).	1. After A.D. 70, Antioch became the center of Christianity. By A.D. 400 over 100,000 Christians lived there.
How does their selection process compare with the way we appoint missionaries today?	
If there are significant differences, which way do you prefer and why?	
2. In what ways was Elymus the Sorcerer (v. 8) like or unlike Simon the magician? (Acts 8)	2. The change of Saul's name to Paul (v. 9) indicates no spiritual or theological change in the man. Saul was his Hebrew name; Paul, his Greek name. The latter was apparently better suited to the Gentile context of his ministry.
3. What was the ultimate outcome of Paul's encounter with Elymus? (v. 12)	

B. HOW TO PREACH ABOUT THE RESURRECTION *(Acts 13:13-52)*.   In the synagogue located at Antioch in Pisidia, Paul and his friends were asked to give a "message of encouragement" to the people, and that is precisely what they did, as this passage reflects. This, the first of Paul's recorded sermons (vv. 16-41), reflects the style of Stephen's preaching.

Explaining the Text	Examining the Text
1. The Pauline pattern of ministry is now beginning to take form—Paul goes first to the synagogue, then to the Gentiles in public places.	1. Read Acts 13:13-52. Turn to the map on page 12. Trace the course of Paul's first missionary journey up into Asia Minor, locating Paphos, Perga, and Antioch of Pisidia. Note their relationships to the geographical references mentioned in our first section of study—Antioch, Seleucia, Cyprus, and Salamis.
	2. To whom was Paul preaching? What specific things had God done for Israel through her history?
	Why do you think Paul took the approach he did in presenting the Gospel to his listeners?
3. The Resurrection dominates Acts 13:30-37. In these eight verses, Paul preaches New Testament resurrection from Old Testament passages.	3. In verse 33 of this passage, Paul quotes from Psalm 2. What is the significance of Paul's quoting from this psalm? (Compare it with 13:8, noting carefully the word *son.*)
4. Notice the elements of the Gospel contained in verses 28-30 (crucifixion, burial, and resurrection) and verses 39-41 (forgiveness, faith, justification, and repentance).	4. What response was Paul hoping for from his listeners? (vv. 38-41)

Examining the Text	*Explaining the Text*
Diagnose the listeners' reactions to the sermon (vv. 42-52). How does their response compare to what missionaries might find in other cultures today?	

C. HOW TO SERVE GOD AS A TRAVELING WITNESS *(Acts 14)*.   As the missionaries travel southeast on the Via Sebaste, they visit Iconium, Lystra, and then Derbe. In the first few verses of chapter 14, we notice that our missionary team is still going to the synagogue first, still receiving a divided response, and still emphasizing God's grace. The "pilgrim/stranger" motif—so often used in the Gospels—now becomes a New Testament standard. As Jesus warned—his followers would be persecuted, just as He had been.

Examining the Text	*Explaining the Text*
1. Read Acts 14. The missionary journeys described in Acts demand that we take a careful look at the geography. Turn once more to the map on page 12 and follow the apostles' course of travel as they make their way into Iconium, Lystra, Derbe, down to Attalia, and eventually back to Antioch in Syria where their first missionary journey comes to an end at the end of this chapter.	1. Luke seems to offer us "pairs" of Christian leaders in his historical narrative— Peter and John, Barnabas and Saul, Judas and Silas, Barnabas and Mark, Paul and Silas, Silas and Timothy, etc.
2. How did the apostles respond to persecution? (vv. 6-7, 19-22)	
3. What did Paul see in the crippled man besides his physical need? (v. 9) How did the crowds respond to this miracle?	3. There was an ancient legend that told of a visit to this area in South Galatia by Zeus and Hermes. Supposedly, these two gods had once come to earth dressed as men.

Explaining the Text	Examining the Text
	4. Acts 14:15-17 are dramatic verses because of what they tell us about "common grace." After reading these verses over carefully, explain what you think "common grace" is, and give some examples of it.
5. The churches of southern Galatia, visited by the missionaries on their first missionary journey, are the recipients of the Epistle to the Galatians, which was written about A.D. 48, shortly after the trip.	5. What kind of "follow-up" program did Paul and Barnabas have to insure that the work they had done would continue? (vv. 21-23)

D. HOW TO RUN CHURCH BUSINESS MEETINGS (*Acts 15:1-29*). The Judaizers (legalistic Palestinian Jews) held a firm position: "The Gentiles must be circumcised and required to obey the Law of Moses" (14:5b). The majority of the church at Antioch, however—represented by their leaders, Paul and Barnabas—disagreed. Although James presides at the meeting, notice how the various opposition parties, and anyone else who can offer helpful testimony, are all free to speak.

Explaining the Text	Examining the Text
1. This early church business meeting had a one-item agenda: What must Gentiles do to be saved?	1. Read Acts 15:1-29. After quite a bit of discussion, the Jerusalem Council finally settled on four requirements for the Gentiles. What were they? (vv. 20, 29)
	2. Why do you think these particular guidelines were chosen in answer to the pressing question about Gentile salvation?

Examining the Text	*Explaining the Text*
3. What were some of the positive results we see coming out of this Jerusalem Council? (vv. 22-23, 30-35)	3. Toward the end of the second century, Clement of Alexandria called this letter from the Jerusalem Council (vv. 24-29) "the catholic epistle of all the apostles."
4. In what other ways do you think the early church was affected by this crucial decision?	4. Though some have called it rigid, this was actually a very generous decision on the part of the Jerusalem church. It freed the Gospel so that it could flourish among the Gentiles, but it also fixed two factions in the church—the Jewish Christians and the Gentile Christians.

E. HOW TO SELECT LEADERS FOR MINISTRY *(Acts 15:30-41)*. Best known for his midnight duet with Paul in the Philippian jail, Silas (Silvanus) now becomes an associate missionary. He shows us that New Testament leadership is neither prominence nor popularity. Rather, it is submission and service. Silas' dignity in tending to the menial tasks at Jerusalem propels him to consequential ministry throughout Asia Minor.

Examining the Text	*Explaining the Text*
1. Read Acts 15:30-41. Make a list of all the verbs you find in verses 30-35 of this passage. Notice how they describe the ministry activities of the church.	1. The Jerusalem Council took place in approximately A.D. 50.
2. Paul and Barnabas were already on their way back to Antioch and could easily have carried the letter from the Jerusalem Council. But the Council also sent Judas Barsabbas and Silas along (v. 22). Why do you suppose they did that?	

Explaining the Text

3. The word used to describe the disagreement between Paul and Barnabas is *paroxysm*. The word appears only one other time in the New Testament (Heb. 10:24).

Examining the Text

3. What problem arose between Paul and Barnabas?

How do you explain the argument that arose between these two spiritually mature, gifted church leaders?

Why do you think Luke includes this incident in his historical account?

4. Why was Silas a particularly good replacement for Barnabas on the missionary team? (v. 32)

Experiencing the Text

1. Looking back at verses 1-4 of Acts 13, how would you describe the spiritual climate of the church at Antioch? What can local churches today do to capture that same spirit?

2. The "team" focus of missionary ministry is very evident throughout the Book of Acts. What makes team ministry effective and attractive both in the local church and on the foreign mission field?

Experiencing the Text

3. Reread Acts 13:44-46. Assuming we understand what Paul meant when he said, "We now turn to the Gentiles," what implications might that statement have for the church today?

4. What would you say were some of the highlights of the first missionary journey? How did God use Paul and Barnabas? How should their experience both challenge and encourage each of us?

5. How do the four moral guidelines, contained in the letter from the Jerusalem Council, apply to us today? (cf. 15:20)

6. Acts 15:32 implies something about the spiritual gifts of Silas and Judas. What are *your* spiritual gifts? How are you developing and using them for the Lord?

Acts 16–18:22

The Second Missionary Journey

Upon hearing of the Japanese raid on Pearl Harbor, Winston Churchill supposedly remarked, "Now we will win." He had correctly sensed the history-changing nature of the event which would bring the full weight of the United States into World War II and literally change the outcome of that global strife. Paul's famous Macedonian vision—the focal point of this portion of our study—also represents a turning point in history. It appears that Paul intended to follow the Via Sebaste to Ephesus, but that was not God's plan. Closing the door to Bithynia, the Holy Spirit sent the Gospel westward, instead of north to what is now Bulgaria, Romania, and Russia. Furthermore, the Gospel could no longer be contained in Palestine and Asia Minor alone—the message of Christ's crucifixion and resurrection would soon penetrate the heart and core of Greek culture itself.

The record of the ministry at Philippi is an authentic Christian hymn—a hymn of believers in fellowship (Acts 16:11-15), in persecution (16:16-28), and in faith (16:29-34). Indeed, persecution accompanied the missionaries wherever they went. From Philippi in Neapolis they headed southwest, traveling some 33 miles to Amphipolis and another 29 miles further to Thessalonica. From there they journeyed through Berea to Athens in Achaia, and finally on to Corinth, ending their journey on an island off the coast of mainland Greece.

While the first missionary journey showed us penetration and persecution in concert as the Gospel moved through Asia Minor, it was nothing like the direct confrontation between Christianity and pagan culture that was seen as the message of Jesus Christ pierced the darkness of Athens and Corinth.

A. MINISTRY IN MACEDONIA *(Acts 16).*   In the first paragraph of this
passage, Luke closes yet another "act" in his play as he explains that the
first-journey churches "were strengthened in the faith and grew daily in
numbers" (16:5). Now he is prepared to open a broad, new vista in which
he, a Gentile, has personal interest. The flow of the Gospel across the
Hellespont is a dramatic development about which Luke could get genuinely excited.

Examining the Text	*Explaining the Text*
1. Read Acts 16. Paul's second missionary journey intro-duces us to several new geographical locations. Using the map on page 12, locate all the towns named in Acts 16 which Paul visited in his travels.	
2. Describe Timothy. (Use the cross-references in your Bible in addition to what's spelled out in Acts 16.)	2. Timothy may very well have been converted as the result of Paul's first mis-sionary journey (cf. 1 Cor. 4:17).
Why do you think the record of Timothy is inserted here?	
Why was it important for Luke to establish at this point Timothy's role in the flow of New Testament events?	
3. What role did the Holy Spirit play in Paul's decision of who should travel and where? (vv. 6-10)	3. In Acts 16, we find the first "we" section in Acts, in-dicating that Luke has joined the missionary team (16:10). The "we" section ends in verse 19, only to re-appear for the second time in Acts 20:5.

Explaining the Text	Examining the Text
4. The first place the missionaries ministered in Macedonia was Philippi. All the events of Acts 16, from verse 13 to the end of the chapter, take place in this city.	4. From the information available to you in this passage, and using a Bible dictionary or encyclopedia, write a description of Philippi. 5. Imagine yourself as the jailer described in Acts 16:25-30. In a sentence or two, explain why you asked for salvation, rather than for physical safety or some other more obvious amenity.

B. GOSPEL AND GREEKS *(Acts 17:1-15)*.   Some 100 miles south of Philippi lay the city of Thessalonica, the capital of Macedonia as well as its largest and most prosperous city. Its population of 200,000 offered Paul an audience potential larger than any he had seen since leaving Antioch of Syria.

Explaining the Text	Examining the Text
	1. Read Acts 17:1-15. What four verbs does Luke use in verses 2-3 to describe the way Paul preached? What do they tell you about Paul's approach to synagogue ministry? What impact did Paul's preaching have on those who were listening? (vv. 4-5) 2. Why do you think the Jews reacted so violently to the Gentiles' acceptance of the Gospel, especially in light of the fact that they themselves had been given the same opportunity but had refused it?

Examining the Text	Explaining the Text
Examining the Text	*Explaining the Text*
3. In Acts 17:11 we read, "Now the Bereans were of more noble character than the Thessalonians, for they received the message with great eagerness and examined the Scriptures every day to see if what Paul said was true." What do you think Paul meant by "more noble character"?	3. Berea was located 50 miles from Thessalonica in another district of Macedonia. Modern-day Berea is what we know as Véroia, Greece.

C. PREACHING TO PAGANS *(Acts 17:16-34)*.   Athens—still a symbol of Western culture today, was the home of Socrates, Plato, and Aristotle. Amazingly enough, this intellectual capital of the realm boasted only a meager population of around 10,000 people. In fact, its population of idols was greater than that of its people. No wonder Paul "was greatly distressed to see that the city was full of idols" (17:16).

Examining the Text	Explaining the Text
Examining the Text	*Explaining the Text*
1. Read Acts 17:16-34. In what ways was this "sermon" of Paul's different from the others he'd preached up to this point?	1. The *Epicureans*, followers of Epicurus (341–270 B.C.), attempted to practice serene detachment, tended to be highly materialistic, and said that the chief end of man was pleasure and happiness. The *Stoics*, on the other hand, were followers of the philosopher Zeno. They tried to live harmoniously with nature, practiced an impersonal fatalism as a philosophy of life, and believed that God was some kind of "world-soul."
Why do you think he began as he did? (cf. vv. 22-23)	
Why did he quote Greek poets and philosophers?	
2. In what ways are major cities in today's world similar to or different from Athens?	

Explaining the Text	Examining the Text
3. Some commentators have suggested that Paul did not really preach the Gospel in Athens. But since verse 34 tells us, "a few men became followers," and then goes on to name a few, we have to assume that the Gospel message was made clear.	3. Several elements of the Gospel clearly appear in Paul's Athenian sermon. Find and list those elements (vv. 29-31).
	4. The turning point in Paul's sermon seems to be his mentioning of the Resurrection (vv. 31-32). Why do you think that particular point got such a rise out of the audience?

D. CONVERTS AT CORINTH *(Acts 18:1-22)*.   Corinth was the capital of Achaia. This city was located 4 miles from the mainland and represented everything sinful in the world. Destroyed by the Romans, Corinth was rebuilt by Caesar in 146 B.C. Nero himself started building the canal which was not completed until 1893, thereby changing Corinth from an island to the Peloponnesian Peninsula.

Explaining the Text	Examining the Text
1. Priscilla and Aquila are mentioned six times in the New Testament. Four of the six times this couple is mentioned in Scripture, Priscilla is named first (Acts 18:2; 18:18-19; 18:26; Rom. 16:3; 1 Cor. 16:19; 2 Tim. 4:19).	1. Read Acts 18:1-22. How would you describe the relationship between the Apostle Paul and Priscilla and Aquila? (See the cross-references in *Explaining the Text #1.*)
	In what ways are Priscilla and Aquila models of Christian character for us today?
	What characterized their lives and ministry?

Examining the Text

2. When Paul and his fellow missionaries were driven out of the synagogue (cf. 18:7-8), or for some other reason chose to leave it, where did they often go?

Explaining the Text

2. Gallio's decision not to settle the dispute between the Jews and Paul in court (18:15) was very important because it identified Christianity as a *religio licita*—a legitimate branch of a legal religion. This was a precedent-setting verdict in the Roman Empire.

3. What factors do you think figured strongly into the early Christians' choice of a meeting place?

Experiencing the Text

1. Timothy is a good example of the important role godly parents play in the lives of their children. How can we raise spiritual sons and daughters like Timothy? (Look at Acts 16:1-5, 2 Timothy 1:1-7, and 1 Timothy 1:18-20 before answering.)

2. Consider the membership of the congregation at Philippi—Luke, Lydia, the jailer and his family, and a slave girl. What are some practical lessons you can learn from their lives? (Jot down at least two ideas.)

3. Think about the role of "prominent women" in the New Testament (Acts 17:4, 34; 18:2). What role have women played in your church? How have they been encouraged to serve God there?

Experiencing the Text

4. The Bereans apparently loved to study the Bible (17:11). How can we teach people to genuinely love Bible study? How can *you* develop more of a love for God's Word?

5. Priscilla and Aquila were so close to the Apostle Paul that they encouraged and supported him in three different cities over a 16-year period. Who is your pastor's helper, encourager—the person he can lean on? How might you be able to be some of these things to him?

6. Acts 18:18-22 emphasizes no fewer than three times the importance of keeping a promise. (Paul fulfills the requirements of a vow at Cenchrea [v. 18]; Paul promises to return to Ephesus "if it is God's will" [v. 21]; and Paul keeps his word to the church at Antioch by going back to offer a full report of the second journey [v. 22].) Why is it important for Christians to keep promises they make? Are there any promises you need to make good on? When will you do it?

Acts 18:23–21:19

The Third Missionary Journey

A young lady applied to a certain college during her senior year in high school. Upon receiving the packet of application forms, she noticed one question in particular. It asked, "Are you a leader?" Pondering her high school activities for a while, she finally decided to answer the question directly and honestly and, at the risk of being rejected by a college which was apparently looking for students who had leadership potential, she responded, "No." Three weeks later the postman delivered to her a letter which radiated an especially warm tone. The admissions director of the college responded, "A study of our application forms shows we have 1,452 leaders in our entering class this fall—they'll need at least one follower—welcome!"

The Book of Acts is about leaders and followers. More precisely, it is about followers who became leaders and who were able to lead because they knew how to follow. In this study, we see again the integrity of the leaders in Acts as Luke paints for us pictures of Apollos and the Ephesian elders. And he adds a few more details to his earlier portraits of Priscilla and Aquila and continues to flesh-out the life and ministry of the little apostle from Tarsus—Paul.

One of the major themes running through Acts 18:23–21:19 is Paul's willingness to live out his faith day by day. Historically, the time of Luke's writing here is approximately the summer of A.D. 53, and the third missionary journey is underway. How many crises there have been in the life of the Apostle Paul. How many times he has stared at death or been faced with decisions of historic consequence. Yet he plods on, trusting his destiny to the hands of his Heavenly Father day after day.

> There is a time we know not when,
> A place we know not where.
> That marks the destiny of men
> To glory and despair.

A. APOLLOS: MODEL OF EVANGELISM *(Acts 18:23-28)*.   Eight or nine months after returning from his second missionary journey, the Apostle Paul plans to set out one more time, for the purpose of "strengthening all the disciples" (18:23). Meanwhile, a new personality breaks onto the Christian scene—a brilliant Alexandrian by the name of Apollos, who evidently possessed "a thorough knowledge of the Scriptures" (18:24). Yet he was deficient in his New Testament theology and had to be taken in hand by faithful lay leaders, Priscilla and Aquila, who "explained to him the way of God more adequately" (18:26). In this passage we see that Christian leadership is more than just enthusiasm.

Examining the Text

1. Read Acts 18:23-28. Apollos of Alexandria breaks onto the stage of the early church with scarcely a warning. Make a list of everything this passage tells us about Apollos.

2. In what way was Apollos' knowledge of the Scriptures inadequate?

    What might Luke mean when he says that Apollos knew "only the baptism of John"?

3. Apollos was a model evangelist in a number of ways. What elements of his ministry do you think we could incorporate into our churches today to improve our evangelistic efforts?

Explaining the Text

1. Alexandria, the second largest city in the Roman Empire, was established in 332 B.C. and was named for Alexander the Great. At this great cultural center, the Nile met the Mediterranean Sea to form the chief grain port of the empire. More than 150,000 tons of grain were sent to Rome from Alexandria each year.

B. EPHESUS: CAPITAL OF ASIA *(Acts 19)*.   Notice that the Christian message is again referred to in this chapter as "the Way" (v. 9). Throughout the chapter, and throughout Paul's ministry in Ephesus, we see confusion about the Way (vv. 1-7); conviction concerning the Way (vv. 8-22); and conflict over the Way (vv. 23-41). Ephesus, the church John addresses so tenderly at the beginning of Revelation 2, was encased in yet another of those urban sin centers, which were so common to Paul's world and to ours.

Explaining the Text	*Examining the Text*
1. Ephesus was the capital of Asia, a center of trade, and a focal point for tourists and pilgrims. Though in decline, Ephesus was still dominated by the temple of Artemis (Greek) or Diana (Latin), a structure four times larger than the Parthenon and one of the seven wonders of the ancient world.	1. Read Acts 19. This chapter contains five or six geographical references. Locate these points on the map on page 12.
	2. From verses 1-7 of Acts 19, try to determine what the disciples at Ephesus believed, and what they did not yet know about New Testament truth. Write a brief summary.
	3. Notice the parallel between Acts 19:5-7 and what we have seen in the earlier chapters of Acts. How was the presence of the Holy Spirit made evident to this group of believers?
	Why do you think God chose to send the Holy Spirit again in visible, physical form?

Examining the Text	*Explaining the Text*
4. During this phase of Paul's ministry, he may have seen some of the "best of times," but also some of the "worst of times." Imagine yourself in the Apostle Paul's shoes at the time of the Acts 19 happenings and write a short journal entry, highlighting the main events that took place.	4. Paul sets a new record in Ephesus—he spends three months preaching in the synagogue without a riot erupting. His total length of ministry there probably lasted somewhere between two and three years (approximately A.D. 53-56). During this time, churches were founded near Colosse, Laodicea, and Hierapolis.

C. TROAS: MIRACLE AT MIDNIGHT *(Acts 20:1-12).*   Paul is "on the road again," this time heading east toward home. You will recall how he had stopped in Troas briefly on his second missionary journey (16:8-11) where he had received his historic Macedonian vision. Now Paul hopes to find Titus who is supposed to bring him a report of the Corinthian churches (2 Cor. 2:12-13; 7:5-16). Already prominent in Paul's mind because of the Macedonian call, Troas takes on new significance in connection with the Eutychus episode.

Examining the Text	*Explaining the Text*
1. Read Acts 20:1-12. Notice the interesting list of companions the Apostle Paul has with him on this leg of the journey (vv. 4-6). Note also Luke's careful recording of their hometowns. (List your observations below.)	1. Macedonia has reference to northern Greece where scholars believe Paul might possibly have spent as long as a year and a half. From here he wrote 2 Corinthians 7:5-16. He may also have traveled as far north as modern Yugoslavia.
Why do you think Luke makes such a point of mentioning those who participated in this special group?	

Explaining the Text

Examining the Text

2. From what you read in verses 1-2, what would you say is one of the main purposes of this phase of Paul's journey?

3. The incident of Eutychus' nap during Paul's long sermon probably joins the stories of Paul's being turned away at Jerusalem (Acts 9) and Peter at the door (Acts 12) as one of the top ten favorite early church stories.

3. Some commentators would suggest that verse 10 implies that Eutychus never really died. Rather he was just thought to be dead by his friends. What do you think? Was this a genuine resurrection miracle? Why or why not?

Why do you think Luke included this episode in his narrative?

D. MILETUS: CHALLENGE TO CHURCH LEADERS *(Acts 20:13-38)*. This may well be one of the most loved passages in the New Testament, especially by pastors and church leaders. After Luke's introductory comments in verses 13-16, Paul launches into his own personal testimony with respect to his relationship with the Ephesian church (vv. 17-24). He goes on to explain their personal responsibility in protecting the unity of the body and genuinely ministering to the church or churches at Ephesus (vv. 25-31). And finally, he offers his own life and ministry as a personal example of how to serve God and maintain integrity in ministry throughout one's life (vv. 32-38).

Explaining the Text

Examining the Text

1. In verse 17, Paul calls the "elders" *(presbuteroi)* together and, later in verse 28, refers to the same group of people as "overseers" *(episkopoi)*. Many believe these are interchangeable terms for the same office of which pastor would also be a part.

1. Read Acts 20:13-38. As an effective leader should, Paul walked in the way of the Lord. Identify several "marks" of Jesus on Paul's ministry (vv. 17-22, 31-38).

Examining the Text	*Explaining the Text*
2. Think about Paul's letters to the different New Testament churches. In what ways does this section (vv. 22-34 in particular) sound like those epistles?	

E. JERUSALEM: DETERMINING GOD'S WILL *(Acts 21:1-19).* This third "we" section puts Luke back in the missionary party once again (21:1). In these nineteen verses, Luke describes Paul's progress toward Jerusalem (vv. 1-9) and then the prophecy of Agabus (vv. 10-16). The passage ends with Paul's greetings and report to the elders (vv. 17-19), carried out with a brief official visit to Jerusalem and then the appropriate return to the sending church at Antioch.

Examining the Text	*Explaining the Text*
1. Read Acts 21:1-19. Why do you think Paul was in such a hurry to get to Jerusalem? (Compare Romans 9:1-5 with Acts 20:22-24 and 21:12-16.)	1. Here again we encounter Philip, the evangelist, whom we met twenty years earlier in the Book of Acts (8:5-40). Philip's four unmarried daughters may have been a good source of information for Luke because of their familiarity with church leaders from the earliest days.
2. In verse 14, what do you think the people meant when they said to Paul, "The Lord's will be done"?	2. Commentators are hopelessly divided on Paul's decision to go to Jerusalem. One writes, "I firmly believe Paul was wrong in this. He was saying, 'My will be done!'" Another disagrees: "Paul's determination to go to Jerusalem came from an inward spiritual constraint that could not be set aside."

Experiencing the Text

1. When Priscilla and Aquila heard Apollos preach, they recognized a deficiency in his "theological education" and tutored/discipled him in the Scriptures. How have you been discipled personally so that your knowledge of Scripture and faith in God has been strengthened?

2. Reread Acts 19:17-22. Here we see the Christians renouncing openly all forms of spiritism as a means of separating themselves from sin. What implications do you see in that action for Christians today? What are some ways in which we need to avoid the influence of spirits of evil in our society?

3. *Encouragement* is a key word in Acts 20. In what ways have you been encouraged by other Christians? Are *you* an encouraging Christian? How can you practice the ministry of encouragement this week?

4. In our churches we sometimes sing, "Blest be the tie that binds...." In Acts 20:13-38 Paul shows obvious concern for the unity of the body of Christ at Ephesus. Name some things you can do to implement and encourage body unity in your church.

5. Though not a commonly known verse, Acts 21:5 describes a most touching scene: the believers as families knelt on the beach to pray and say good-bye to Paul and his associates. What does it mean when we say that the church is a "family of families"? What is your church doing to build stronger families?

Acts 21:20–23:35

Arrest in Jerusalem

In April, 1981, CBS debuted an exciting two-part miniseries on the lives, ministries, and deaths of the Apostles Peter and Paul. Rerun many times since then, this four-hour drama is very well done with superb acting and an unexpected faithfulness to the text of Scripture at most points.

There are, however, a number of inaccuracies in the presentation. One such inaccuracy portrays the Christians as a small, harassed group of people who hid in rooms and grottos during the early years of the church. This is hardly consistent with the bold preaching of Peter and John as early as chapter 4 of Acts, the testimony of Stephen in the synagogue, and the record of thousands of believers in Jerusalem, Judea, and Samaria during the early years of the church.

What the TV producers failed to realize, or at least failed to portray, is that the reality of persecution, increasing in intensity throughout the fourth and fifth decades of the first century, served only to strengthen the resolve of the believers. That courage is shown most distinctly in the life and ministry of the Apostle Paul, even in his declining years. Even though he is arrested in chapter 21 of Acts, the book goes on to describe the impact of his life and witness in chains for seven more chapters. Perhaps this is Luke's way of paying tribute to such an amazing servant of Jesus Christ.

A. PRAISE IN THE CHURCH *(Acts 21:20-26)*.   Back in Jerusalem, Paul is once again thrust into the argument and conflict between law and grace. The Jews are willing to affirm his Gentile mission and accept the offering he brings from the Gentile churches; Paul is willing to reciprocate by identifying with four men in this whole vow incident. Included in the bargain, however, is a reminder that this request in no way undermines the agreement made earlier (cf. Acts 21:25; 15:20, 29).

Examining the Text

1. Read Acts 21:17-26. Paul has just returned from his third missionary journey and been received warmly by the brethren at Jerusalem. Then comes the accusation. Of what is Paul accused? (v. 21)

Was their accusation accurate? If not, what *did* Paul teach the Jews living among the Gentiles?

2. How did Paul respond to the accusation? (vv. 24-26)

Some people believe Paul compromised his gospel of grace on this occasion, though Scripture does not seem to support that view. After reviewing Acts 15, suggest some reasons why Paul might have chosen to involve himself in this vow.

Explaining the Text

1. The vow spoken of in verse 23 was not a Nazarite vow, which would have taken thirty days to complete. It appears to be a simple act of piety, whereby Paul tries to identify with the Jews in order to minister to them more adequately.

B. PERSECUTION IN THE WORLD *(Acts 21:27-40)*.   The words of Jesus now come into full reality—"No servant is greater than his master. If they persecuted Me, they will persecute you also" (John 15:20). Persecution can take many forms, and the ugly form in which it surfaced in Acts 21:22-40 was "anarchy." Bullies in the streets, taking the law into their own hands, are no better in the eyes of God and no less a threat to society just because their motives originate in religious fervor.

Explaining the Text	*Examining the Text*
1. Gentiles were explicitly forbidden to go beyond the four-and-a-half foot high barrier which separated the court of the Gentiles from the temple proper. The Romans allowed the death penalty for anyone transgressing this law.	1. Read Acts 21:27-40. Anarchy seems to be so prevalent in human society, both in Paul's day and in ours. In what ways do the rioters described in this passage exemplify lawlessness and rebellion?
	Why do you think these people hated Paul so intensely?
2. The central task of any Roman politician or military officer was to preserve the *pax romana* (21:31-34).	2. What is the opposite of anarchy?
	The mob behavior described in this portion of our passage is not the way biblical Christians should respond. How, then, *should* they respond?

C. PREACHING IN THE STREETS *(Acts 22:1-29).*   The word *apologia* is used eight times in the New Testament. Stephen offered an eloquent *apologia* (defense) before the Sanhedrin in Acts 7. Amazingly, Stephen's message began with precisely the same words Paul used here: "Brothers and fathers" (22:1). These two model servants of Christ lived up to the injunction offered by Peter to all Christians, "But in your hearts set apart Christ as Lord. Always be prepared to give an answer to everyone who asks you to give the reason for the hope that you have" (1 Peter 3:15).

Examining the Text	*Explaining the Text*
1. Read Acts 22:1-29. In Acts 22:3-21 we hear Paul giving his own personal testimony, recorded earlier by Luke in Acts 9:1-19. Identify three or four major features of Paul's own salvation story.	1. Paul addressed the crowd in Aramaic and when they heard their own familiar mother tongue, they settled down (22:2).
2. How would you explain Acts 22:16? Was Paul saying that salvation comes by water baptism? (cf. Rom. 2:28-29; Eph. 2:8-9; Phil. 3:4-9)	2. Remember—baptism is an outward sign of God's inward work of grace (1 Cor. 6:11; 1 Peter 3:21).
3. When Paul mentioned the Word *Gentiles*, the crowd instantly exploded in rage (vv. 21-22). Why was this word so offensive to the Jews? (cf. Eph. 2:11-22; 3:2-6; Gal. 3:28)	

Explaining the Text	*Examining the Text*
4. Paul was no stranger to flogging (Acts 16:22-23; 2 Cor. 11:24-25). But this flogging was different. Instead of using a long whip like a slave driver might use, the soldier used a shorter whip embedded with pieces of metal or bones and attached to a strong wooden handle. Paul was faced with an ordeal that could potentially kill him or leave him permanently crippled. This punishment was the same kind of punishment Christ received (Matt. 27:26) at the close of His trial.	4. What question did Paul ask the centurion? Why was such a fuss made over the fact of Paul's Roman citizenship? Why do you think Paul referred to his Roman citizenship on more than one occasion?

D. PLOT IN THE CITY *(Acts 22:30–23:35).* The key thought which runs throughout this portion of our passage is *God is in control of all circumstances.* There is also a key verse—Acts 23:11. Here the Lord speaks directly to Paul and encourages him regarding a future ministry in Rome.

Explaining the Text	*Examining the Text*
1. Ananias, the son of Nedebaeus, served as high priest from A.D. 48-58. He was noted for cruelty, greed, and violence. His own people assassinated him in A.D. 66.	1. Read Acts 22:30–23:35. Notice the dialogue that takes place between Ananias the high priest and Paul (vv. 1-5). In light of what Paul says in verse 3, how would you explain Paul's statement in verse 5? Offer several possible explanations for this seemingly quick change of attitude.
2. This is the fourth vision the Lord gave Paul (cf. 9:4-6; 16:9; 18:9-10; 23:11).	2. How did the Lord comfort and encourage Paul in his time of need? (v. 11) Why do you think the Lord did this?

Examining the Text	Explaining the Text
3. What human means did the Lord use to protect Paul? How has the Lord worked similarly in your life?	
4. Study the letter from Claudis Lycius (vv. 26-30). Explain why you consider his handling of the matter just or unjust.	4. Felix was governor of Judea from A.D. 52-59. The Roman historian Tacitus called him "a master of cruelty and lust who exercised the power of a king with the spirit of a slave."

Experiencing the Text

1. It seems like Paul was constantly faced with the conflict between law and grace. How have you evidenced this tension point in your own Christian experience?

2. Quickly review Acts 21. In what ways is Paul an example of a faithful Christian who can make it through anything because God is with him? (Cite specific instances and list their references.) How far would your own faithfulness and obedience to Christ take you?

3. Jesus warned His followers that they would face persecution even as He had had to do. In what ways is the church today experiencing persecution? How have you as a Christian experienced persecution?

Experiencing the Text

4. The pictures of Paul in Acts 22:1-29—Pharisee, Christian, and prisoner—remind us of the importance of being faithful to our commitments and leaving the problems to God. How can we work these two ideas out practically in our day-to-day living?

5. In Acts 23:11 we see how God's presence comforted and encouraged Paul in his time of need. Name some ways in which the Lord's presence can dispel loneliness, fear, worry, etc. How have you experienced the peace of God's presence in your own life?

6. Apart from verse 11, there is not a great deal of encouragement in chapter 23 of Acts. How do you *know* that God is always in control of all the circumstances of your life?

Acts 24–26

Felix, Festus, and Agrippa

Amnesty International claims that one half of the 157 members of the United Nations hold prisoners. Their estimates suggest there are at least 10,000 prisoners in the U.S.S.R., 2,000 in Poland, 15,000 in Turkey, 10,000 in Africa, 100,000 in Asia, and over 10,000 in South America.

Acts 24–26 affords us an opportunity to view Paul as a political prisoner. None of the three major characters Luke describes in these chapters care at all about justice, freedom, or civil rights. And they certainly have no interest in the gospel of the Resurrection. But in the midst of this selfish, political arena, the Apostle Paul continues to proclaim Christ's message of redeeming grace with distinctive and courageous clarity.

The world rarely assesses value accurately, as we see in this example: A young man received a degree in Zoology from Syracuse University in 1968. He was rejected by several all-American medical schools, and finally enrolled in Bologna, only to drop out two years later. Finally, this young man earned a medical degree from the University of Utah. His name? Robert Jarvik, the surgeon who gave the world its first permanent, artificial heart.

In our passage for this study, Paul stands on trial before the world. And what he teaches us is the values of God—that in order to live, we must be free of the fear of dying.

A. FELIX: POLITICIAN ON THE TAKE *(Acts 24:1-27)*. In Acts 24 we find ourselves in a first-century court of law. Ananias, the religious authority, and Tertullus, the legal authority, present the case for the prosecution (vv. 1-9). Paul responds with the case for the defense (vv. 10-21). Then Felix, representing the civil authority, offers the verdict (vv. 22-27). Unfortunately, his weakness and procrastination show how ill-equipped he is to carry out his task.

Examining the Text	*Explaining the Text*
1. Read Acts 24:1-27. Tertullus makes three specific charges against Paul (vv. 5-8). What are they?	1. Here we see something of Luke's writing style—he gives careful attention to the recording of historical details accurately: *When*—"five days later"; *Where*—"Caesarea"; *Who*—"Ananias the high priest, some of the elders, a lawyer named Tertullus."
2. What answer does Paul give for each of the charges brought against him? (vv. 11-21)	
3. Paul "boils down" to one sentence the real issue of the charges brought against him (v. 21). In one or two words what was that issue?	
4. Verse 22 tells us Felix "was well acquainted with the Way." How do you suppose he knew about Christianity? (v. 24)	4. Drusilla, Felix's wife, was a daughter of Herod Agrippa I and a sister of Herod Agrippa II.
5. Why do you think Paul changed the subject of his conversation with Felix from "faith in Christ Jesus" (v. 24) to "righteousness, self-control, and the judgment to come"? (v. 25)	

B. FESTUS: BOOK SOLDIER FOR ROME *(Acts 25:1-22)*.   Nero is now emperor and Felix has been fired as procurator of Judea. The first five years of Nero's reign were thought by his subjects to be a "golden age." Festus, who succeeded Felix as procurator of Judea is known in history as a just but undistinguished leader. (He carries out the requirements of the system without making himself vulnerable through any significant decisions.) The fuss being made over Jewish theology was totally incomprehensible to him, a Roman governor so Festus, in short, "passes the buck."

Explaining the Text	*Examining the Text*
1. The phrase, "I have not done any wrong to the Jews" (v. 10) would indicate that the charges brought against Paul were civil. Therefore, the present court where Festus represented Caesar was the proper court.	1. Read Acts 25:1-22. Why did Paul refuse to go to Jerusalem for trial? (vv. 10-11)
2. Like his predecessor Felix, Festus does not understand why Paul insists on focusing on the resurrection of Christ whenever he has a discussion with the Jews (vv. 19-20). This one theological issue seems to be at the heart of all Paul's court problems.	2. Why do you think Paul insists on repeating the same message of Jesus Christ—that He died and rose again—time after time?
	What are the implications of this action of Paul's for us in the church today?
	3. What evidence do you find in this passage to support the idea that Paul was trusting in God, not himself, to get him through the various Roman court proceedings?
	4. Based on what you read in this passage, and from what you remember of Paul's previous encounters with his accusers, what would you say was Paul's strategy for handling those who were in a position to judge him?

C. AGRIPPA: PUPPET KING ON A THRONE *(Acts 25:23–26:32).* As the Apostle Paul stands before a king, his courage does not waver, his message does not change, and his conviction does not lessen. In essence he is saying, "I was deeply religious. I was an official fanatic. But then I met Jesus. I became His disciple, and ever since then I have preached His resurrection." To all of that, he receives two political responses—pagan rejection (26:24-27) and religious rejection (26:28-32). But along the way, Paul takes us to the mountain of hope and testimony (v. 29).

Examining the Text	*Explaining the Text*
1. Read Acts 25:23–26:32. From the information you find in this passage, write a description of King Agrippa.	1. This is the longest of all Paul's defenses recorded in Acts (cf. 22:1-21; 23:1-8; 24:10-21; 25:6-11).
2. Paul's innocence is mentioned or alluded to several times in this passage. Find the references and list the verses, noting in each case who is speaking.	
3. Commentators have interpreted Agrippa's response to Paul (v. 28) in numerous ways. What do you think Agrippa was saying to Paul?	
4. What can we learn from the Apostle's proclamation of the Gospel before this Jewish King?	
5. How does Paul's missionary heart reveal itself in verse 29?	

Experiencing the Text

1. The central issue of Paul's personal message is that "Jesus is alive" (24:21). In what ways has that fact changed your life, particularly in relationship to a pagan world?

2. Someone has said, "Not to decide is to decide." And at the end of Acts 24 we find Felix doing just that. Why do you think people put off responding to something as important as the Gospel? How should this tendency toward procrastination affect the way we as Christians approach witnessing?

3. As was noted earlier in the lesson, "In order to live, we need to be free of the fear of dying." What must Christians believe to live life in this way? What values must guide their decisions?

4. In Acts 26:16-18 the Apostle Paul describes his "call" to serve the Lord. Compare this with Isaiah 42:6-7; Jeremiah 1:7-8; and Ezekiel 2:1-3. How has God worked in your life to lead you to what you are currently doing? Or perhaps God is leading you into some new phase of life. How has He been leading?

5. In the first century, Rome had no hospitals or orphanages; they only had crosses and arenas of death. The Gospel closed those arenas and opened missions. What are the social implications of the Gospel for today's world? In other words, what kinds of things should we be doing in addition to proclaiming the message of eternal life?

Acts 27–28

From Caesarea to Rome

Sailing the Mediterranean on an ancient ship was like life itself. Sometimes it was slow. Sometimes the journey was dangerous. At other times it was boringly calm. Occasionally, disaster struck. But always, the trip was bound to be full of surprises.

Such was the case of Paul, who boarded a ship in Caesarea in the fall of A.D. 59. Bible historians tell us that Luke has given his readers a very accurate account of ancient history. In the first verse of Acts 27 we find the fourth "we" section in the book, reminding us that Luke is giving us an eyewitness account of all that's happening. And throughout the journey, the imprisonment, the shipwreck, and the trial, Luke reports that Paul remains a serene and joyful Christian.

Paul's life and philosophy stand in stark contrast to the attitudes of many who have suffered. Robert Louis Stevenson, for example, despite his literary brilliance, wrote shortly before his death by consumption, "For fourteen years I have not had a day's health. I have awakened sick and gone to bed weary. I have written in bed, written in hemorrhages, written in sickness, written though torn by coughing, written when my head swam from weakness. . . . My battlefield is this dingy inglorious one of the bed and the medicine bottle." Compare his mournful and depressing words with those Luke records about the Apostle Paul in the last verse of Acts: "Boldly and without hindrance he preached the kingdom of God and taught about the Lord Jesus Christ" (28:31).

Acts contains few details about Paul's work in Rome. But from what we read in the Epistles, we surmise that Paul *did* stand trial before Caesar and that he expected to be exonerated. Whether or not he would actually be released Luke could not say, but he clearly intends to emphasize victory at the end of his report to Theophilus.

A. VOYAGE TO ROME *(Acts 27).* Navigation in this part of the Mediterranean was always dangerous after September 14 and usually impossible after November 11. Nevertheless, the ship's sailors set out sometime in early October only to run smack into a "northeaster" (v. 14), which eventually led to the shipwreck described in verses 27-44.

Examining the Text	*Explaining the Text*
1. Trace Paul's sea voyage on the map on page 12. Who was traveling with Paul?	1. A quick glance at the map on page 12 will show you how the ship stayed close to the long east coast of the island of Cyprus because of westerly winds. At Myra, the most illustrious city in Lycia, the passengers changed to a larger grain ship, hoping to meet the weather on its own terms.
2. Describe the officer in charge (vv. 1-3). Why do you think the officer in charge treated Paul as he did?	
3. God's hand was certainly on Paul and his friends during this trip. Find and list several examples of God's care found in Acts 27.	3. Paul's behavior on board ship is a marvelous demonstration of "emergent leadership." The prisoner becomes the commander and as a prophet of God, rescues every man on board. Despite Luke's elaborate description of anchors, ropes, swimming, and planks, he surely intends for us to see in all this a clear demonstration of God's supernatural deliverance.

B. ARRIVAL IN ROME *(Acts 28:1-16)*. Paul's problems are just beginning when he washes up on shore at Malta. While helping with the chores he is bitten by a poisonous snake, taken to be a god, and then expected to work with Luke in miraculously healing people across the island. Finally there is genuine welcome at Rome. Paul and his traveling companions are greeted warmly by brothers in Puteoli and again at the Forum of Appius (a market town 43 miles from Rome) and the Three Taverns (33 miles from Rome).

Explaining the Text

1. Malta, known as Melita by the Greeks and Romans, means "a place of refuge." This island was 18 miles long, 8 miles wide, and lay some 58 miles south of Sicily.

Examining the Text

1. Trace the "last leg" of Paul's journey from Malta to Rome on your map (vv. 11-16).

2. What kind of reception did Paul and his comrades receive from the islanders of Malta?

3. In this passage, we don't read that Paul was *preaching* the Gospel to those who lived on the island, but we do observe him *practicing* the Gospel. Cite several specific examples of "social work" Paul was doing while on Malta.

In this instance, why do you think Paul concentrated on the "social" aspect of the Gospel rather than on the "defense" aspect?

4. In verse 14, Luke writes, "And so we came to Rome." How do you think Paul felt at that particular moment?

Having been faced with so many obstacles and hardships along the way, what do you think kept Paul going?

C. WITNESS TO ROME *(Acts 28:17-31)*. Paul's formula for sharing the Gospel has not changed—to the Jew first and then to the Greek. This passage begins with the leaders of the Jews assembling and Paul explaining his position to them. The Jewish community in Rome seems to be genuinely ignorant of the Gospel and of Paul's previous ministry. By verse 25 we read, "They disagreed among themselves and began to leave," which is Paul's signal to turn to the Gentiles, and he does this immediately (28:28). The last word of the Greek text of Acts is *akolutos* ("without hindrance"). This is Luke's way of telling us how God has prepared the way for the Gospel to go forth freely, even to the heart of the Roman Empire.

Examining the Text	*Explaining the Text*
1. Read Acts 28:17-31. In Rome, Paul continued to follow his normal pattern of speaking to the Jews before speaking to the Gentiles. How are the leaders of the Jews in Rome different from those Paul had encountered in Jerusalem? (vv. 21-25)	
2. Paul claimed to be bound with chains "because of the hope of Israel" (v. 20). To what is he referring?	2. Here Paul quotes Isaiah 6:9-10 to explain Israel's stubbornness and to show how God's providence has brought redemption.
3. Think through the highlights of Paul's life and ministry. In light of what you read in Acts 28:31, how was Christ's commission (Acts 1:8) fulfilled through Paul?	3. Acts 28:31 seems to be a ringing final declaration of Luke's account—the Gospel is being proclaimed and God's soverign will is proceeding "without hindrance."

Experiencing the Text

1. In the spiritual sense, Christians know that disaster is coming to the world, just as Paul knew that the storm would hit the ship. In view of that knowledge, what is our responsibility as Christians to the world?

2. In Acts 27, we see clearly how God took care of Paul. How has God's care been demonstrated in your own life? (List specific examples.)

3. Paul is a marvelous example of the "*inter*dependent" Christian (versus either the *dependent* or *in*dependent Christian). That is, people depended on him and he depended on others. Describe how that idea should work within the context of a local body of believers today.

4. Paul was encouraged by the "brothers" (28:14-15). In what ways are you actively and practically attempting to encourage others?

5. In Acts 27–28, we see that the key to deliverance and victory is abject obedience to God. In what ways are you practicing strict obedience to God and His Word? How can you teach this type of obedience to your own children, to a Sunday School class, or share it in some other way with people?

6. How have these twelve studies in Acts affected your life? List at least five ideas, attitudes, or actions which have changed as the result of studying Acts.